Mies van der Rohe

Mies van der Rohe

teNeues

Editor in chief:
Paco Asensio

Editor and original texts:
Aurora Cuito

Photographs:
Rui Morais de Sousa

English translation:
William Bain

German translation:
Inken Wolthaus

French translation:
Michel Ficerai

Italian translation:
Grazia Suffriti

Art direction:
Mireia Casanovas Soley

Graphic design / Layout:
Emma Termes Parera and Soti Mas-Bagà

Published worldwide by teNeues Publishing Group
(except Spain, Portugal and South-America):

teNeues Verlag GmbH + Co. KG
Am Selder 37, 47906 Kempen, Germany
Tel.: 0049-(0)2152-916-0
Fax: 0049-(0)2152-916-111

teNeues Publishing Company
16 West 22nd Street, New York, N.Y., 10010, USA
Tel.: 001-212-627-9090
Fax: 001-212-627-9511

teNeues Publishing UK Ltd.
Aldwych House, 71/91 Aldwych
London WC2B 4HN, UK
Tel.: 0044-1892-837-171
Fax: 0044-1892-837-272

teNeues France S.A.R.L.
140, rue de la Croix Nivert
75015 Paris, France
Tel.: 0033-1-5576-6205
Fax: 0033-1-5576-6419

www.teneues.com

Editorial project:

© 2002 LOFT Publications
Domènech 9, 2-2
08012 Barcelona. Spain
Tel.: 0034 93 218 30 99
Fax: 0034 93 237 00 60
e-mail: loft@loftpublications.com
www.loftpublications.com

Printed by:
Gráficas Anman. Sabadell. Spain

May 2002

Die Deutsche Bibliothek – CIP-Einheitsaufnahme
Ein Titeldatensatz für diese Publikation ist bei der Deutschen Bibliothek erhältlich.

ISBN: 3-8238-5581-6

The extraordinary coherence of the work of Ludwig Mies van der Rohe (1886 – 1969) bases itself on the solid intellectual and theoretical framework that subtends it. In spite of not having studied architecture at any university, his professional training was rigorous and allowed him to develop and transmit a set of building principles that have become indispensable to understanding and practicing modern architecture. Mies began working in the family workshop as a stone worker. There, he gained an acute sense of how to select materials, textures, and finishes. He earned access to the studio of the prestigious architect Peter Behrens, who put him in contact with the advanced building techniques of the time and introduced him to Walter Gropius. Mies would, eventually, succeed Gropius as the director of the Bauhaus, the school of greatest artistic influence in Europe between the world wars. After setting up an office in Berlin, Mies left his native Germany in 1937 and moved to the United States. Here, he continued his teaching and his work acquired a greater structural and functional clarity. Mies discovered the perfect balance between technical precision and creative artistic freedom, and this made him one of the great masters of twentieth-century architecture.

Die außergewöhnliche Kohärenz der Bauten von Ludwig Mies van der Rohe (1886 – 1969) stützt sich auf seine solide intellektuelle und theoretische Struktur. Obwohl er keine Universitäten zum Studium der Architektur besucht hatte, verfügte er über eine solide berufliche Ausbildung, die ihm erlaubte, konstruktive Prinzipien ausreifen zu lassen und zu verbreiten, die aus dem Verständnis und Praxis der modernen Architektur nicht mehr wegzudenken sind. Er begann seine Arbeit in der elterlichen Werkstatt für Steinbearbeitung und erwarb dort eine bemerkenswerte Sensibilität bei der Auswahl von Materialien, Texturen und Gestaltung von Oberflächen. Er ging bei dem berühmten Architekten Peter Behrens in die Lehre, der ihn mit den modernen Bau-Techniken der Epoche bekannt machte und ihn Walter Gropius vorstellte, dessen Nachfolger als Leiter des Bauhaus er wurde, einer Schule, die im Europa zwischen den Weltkriegen den größten künstlerischen Einfluss ausübte. Nachdem er sich in Berlin ein eigenes Büro eingerichtet hatte, verließ er 1937 Deutschland und zog in die USA, wo er seine Lehrarbeit wieder aufnahm und seine Werke größere strukturelle und funktionelle Klarheit gewannen. Mies fand das perfekte Gleichgewicht zwischen technischer Präzision und künstlerischer kreativer Freiheit, wodurch er zu einem der großen Meister der Architektur des 20. Jahrhunderts wurde.

L'extraordinaire cohérence de l'œuvre de Ludwig Mies van der Rohe (1886 – 1969) se fonde sur la solide structure intellectuelle et théorique qui la soutient. Bien qu'il n'ait suivi aucun cursus universitaire en architecture, sa formation professionnelle fut solide et lui permit de gérer et de diffuser des principes de construction, devenus indispensables à la compréhension et à la pratique de l'architecture moderne. Il commença à travailler au sein de l'atelier familial de taille de pierres, où il acquit une sensibilité prononcée dans le choix des matériaux, des textures et des finitions. Il accéda à la prestigieuse étude de l'architecte Peter Behrens qui le mit en contact avec les techniques de constructions les plus avancées pour l'époque et lui présenta Walter Gropius. Il allait succéder à ce dernier à la direction du Bauhaus, l'école de majeure influence artistique de l'Europe de l'entre-deux guerres. Apres avoir créé son propre bureau à Berlin, il quitta l'Allemagne en 1937 pour les États-Unis. Il put continuer ainsi son travail d'enseignement et son œuvre acquit une plus grande clarté structurelle et fonctionnelle. Mies rencontra l'équilibre parfait entre la précision technique et la liberté de création artistique, se convertissant ainsi en l'un des grands maîtres de l'architecture du XXème siècle.

La straordinaria coerenza dell'opera di Ludwig Mies van der Rohe (1886 – 1969) è basata sulla solida struttura intellettuale e teorica che la regge. Nonostante non avesse svolto studi di architettura in nessuna università, la sua formazione professionale fu solida e gli permise di sviluppare e diffondere dei principi costruttivi divenuti imprescindibili per comprendere e praticare l'architettura moderna. Cominciò lavorando nella bottega famigliare di lavorazione della pietra, dove acquisì una marcata sensibilità sulla scelta dei materiali, delle loro composizioni e finiture. Entrò nello studio del prestigioso architetto Peter Behrens, che lo mise in contatto con le avanzate tecniche costruttive dell'epoca e gli presentò Walter Gropius, al quale sarebbe seguito come direttore della Bauhaus, la scuola con maggior influenza artistica dell'Europa tra le due guerre. Dopo aver montato il proprio studio a Berlino, lasciò la Germania natale nel 1937 e si trasferì negli Stati Uniti, dove continuò il lavoro di docenza e la sua opera acquistò una maggior chiarezza strutturale e funzionale. Mies ha trovato l'equilibrio perfetto tra la precisione tecnica e la libertà della creazione artistica, per questo è divenuto uno dei grandi maestri dell'architettura del XX° secolo.

Weissenhof Siedlung Apartments

Weissenhof, 20
Stuttgart, Germany
1925–1927

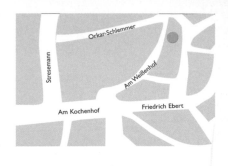

In 1925, Mies made a first urbanistic study for an apartment complex to be built on the outskirts of Stuttgart. The project, which set the blocks on a hillside, was harshly criticized by the classical architects of the time, who called it excessively formalist. In the face of the rejection, Mies approached the project in a more conventional way, organizing around a central space and changing the curves into a rectilinear piece. The apartment complex was designed by the most prestigious architects of the moment, people such as Walter Gropius, Hans Scharoun, Le Corbusier, and Peter Behrens. Mies took charge of one of the main buildings, developed on four stories, with a stairway leading to two apartments per story. It was the first building the architect designed with a steel frame, and he distributed the domestic spaces in a more flexible way that included numerous varied bays. With the exception of the kitchen and bathroom walls, all the perpendicular separators are moveable, thus increasing the versatility of the interiors.

1925 machte Mies einen ersten städteplanerischen Entwurf für einen Wohnkomplex, der an der Peripherie von Stuttgart entstehen sollte. Das Projekt, nach dem Blöcke rund um einen Hügel errichtet werden sollten, wurde von den klassizistischen Architekten dieser Zeit sehr kritisiert, weil es zu formalistisch erschien. Angesichts dieser Zurückweisung ging Mies konventioneller vor und ordnete den Komplex um einen zentralen Bereich herum an, wobei er den gebogenen Achsen durch Anwendung einer rechtwinkligen Geometrie einen geradlinigen Verlauf gab. Die Apartmentblöcke wurden von den zu dieser Zeit berühmtesten Architekten entworfen, wie z. B. von Walter Gropius, Hans Scharoun, Le Corbusier und Peter Behrens. Mies übernahm eines der größten Hauptgebäude mit vier Stockwerken und einer Treppe, die zu zwei Wohnungen pro Etage führt. Dies war das erste Gebäude, das der Architekt mit Stahlkonstruktion entwarf, womit er eine größere Flexibilität in der Aufteilung der häuslichen Räume und eine Vielzahl von verschiedenen Zwischenräumen erreichte. Mit Ausnahme der Wände von Küchen und Badezimmern bestehen alle vertikalen Abtrennungen aus beweglichen Trennwänden, die eine vielseitige Verwendungsmöglichkeit der Innenbereiche gewähren.

En 1925, Mies mena à bien la première proposition urbanistique pour un ensemble de logements destinés à la périphérie de Stuttgart. Le projet, disposant les blocs autour d'une colline, fut l'objet de nombre de critiques par les architectes classiques de l'époque, qui le taxèrent d'excessivement formaliste. Face à la réaction de rejet, Mies aborda la commande de façon très conventionnelle, organisant l'ensemble autour d'un espace central et convertissant les axes courbes en une trame rectiligne dominée par une géométrie orthogonale. Les blocs d'appartements furent conçus par les architectes les plus prestigieux du moment, tels Walter Gropius, Hans Scharoun, Le Corbusier et Peter Behrens. Mies se chargea d'un des bâtiments principaux, développé sur quatre niveaux, avec un escalier offrant accès à deux logements par étage. Il s'agit de la première construction à structure d'acier créée par l'architecte. Elle lui permit d'imposer une distribution des espaces domestiques plus flexible et d'offrir nombre d'espaces diversifiés. De plus, et hormis les murs des cuisines et des salles de bain, toutes les autres partitions verticales sont constituées de cloisons mobiles augmentant la versatilité de l'intérieur.

Nel 1925 Mies portò a termine una prima proposta urbanistica per un gruppo di alloggi che sarebbero stati costruiti nella periferia di Stuttgart. Il progetto, che collocava i blocchi intorno ad una collina, fu molto criticato dagli architetti classicisti dell'epoca, che lo tacciarono di eccessivo formalismo. Di fronte a tale rifiuto Mies affrontò l'incarico in modo più convenzionale, organizzando l'insieme intorno ad uno spazio centrale, trasformando gli assi curvi in una trama rettilinea dominata da una geometria ortogonale. I blocchi di appartamenti furono progettati dagli architetti più prestigiosi del momento, come Walter Gropius, Hans Scharoun, Le Corbusier e Peter Behrens. Mies s'incaricò di uno degli edifici principali, sviluppato su quattro piani, con una scala che dà accesso a due alloggi per piano. Era la prima costruzione che l'architetto progettava con struttura d'acciaio, ed ottenne in questo modo che la distribuzione degli spazi della casa fosse più flessibile e che potessero esserci numerosi e svariati vani. Inoltre, eccetto le pareti della cucina e dei bagni, tutte le altre partiture verticali sono divisorie mobili, che aumentano la versatilità dell'interno.

German Pavilion

Av. Marqués de Comillas s/n, Montjuïc
Barcelona, Spain
1928–1929

In the summer of 1928, Mies was named artistic director of design for all the German delegations attending the International Exposition in Barcelona. His relations with Georg von Schnitzel, the German Reich's general commissary, and with the textile industrialists of the time, were decisive in his receiving this position. Design needed to restore to Germany its loss of prestige after the First World War. Design had to serve as the framework for diplomatic activities and social acts in keeping with a trade fair promoting commerce and international relations. The pavilion raised, on a rectangular dais of 212 feet, was delineated by a perimeter wall a metallic framework covered with marble. It was separate from the structural system of columns, hence reducible to a thickness of seven inches. The canvas roof appeared very light because it was seated on only eight cruciform steel columns. The shallow ponds covering part of the surface area, the glass doors, and the marble walls created a great variety of reflections of the building. It was dismantled shortly after the close of the exhibit, and reconstructed by Ignasi de Solà-Morales at the end of the 1980.

Im Sommer 1928 wurde Mies zum künstlerischen Konstruktionsleiter für alle deutschen Firmen auf der Weltausstellung in Barcelona ernannt. Entscheidend für diesen Auftrag waren seine Beziehungen zu Georg von Schnitzel, dem Reichs-Generalkommissar, und zu den Textilfabrikanten dieser Zeit. Das Design sollte Deutschland das nach dem 1. Weltkrieg verlorene Ansehen wieder zurückgeben und als Rahmen für die diplomatischen Aktivitäten und gesellschaftlichen Ereignisse dienen, die eine Messe zur Förderung der Wirtschaft und der internationalen Beziehungen mit sich bringt. Der Pavillon erhob sich auf einem rechteckigen Podium von 56,5 Metern und wurde begrenzt von Mauern aus einem marmorverkleideten, vom strukturellen System der Pfeiler getrennten Metallgerüst, wodurch ihre Stärke auf 18 Zentimeter reduziert werden konnte. Die auf acht kreuzförmigen Stahlpfeilern abgestützte Dachplatte vermittelte Leichtigkeit. Die flachen Teiche auf einem Teil der Fläche, die Verglasungen und Marmorwände riefen in dem Gebäude vielfältige Spiegelungen hervor; nach der Ausstellung wurde es abgebrochen und Ende der achtziger Jahre von Ignasi de Solà-Morales wieder aufgebaut.

Au cours de l'été 1928, Mies fut nommé directeur artistique de la création pour l'ensemble des délégations allemandes lors de l'Exposition International de Barcelone. Ses relations avec Georg von Schnitzel, commissaire général du Reich, et avec les industriels du textile de l'époque furent décisives dans sa nomination. La conception devait retrouver le prestige perdu de l'Allemagne après la première guerre mondiale. Il devait, en outre, servir de cadre aux activités diplomatiques et aux événements mondains propres d'une exposition promouvant le commerce et les relations internationales. Le pavillon fut édifié sur un podium rectangulaire de 56,5 mètres et délimité par des murs constitués d'une armature métallique recouverte de marbre, libres par rapport au système structurel de piliers, réduisant de ce fait son épaisseur à 18 centimètres. La couverture du toit paraît très légère, car elle s'appuie sur huit piliers cruciformes en acier. Les étangs peu profonds, occupant une partie de la superficie, les fermetures en verre et les murs en marbre créent une grande variété de reflets dans l'immeuble, démantelé peu après l'exposition et reconstruit par Ignasi de Solà-Morales à la fin des années 80.

Nell'estate del 1928, Mies fu nominato direttore artistico della progettazione di tutte le delegazioni tedesche nell'Esposizione Internazionale di Barcellona. Le sue relazioni con Georg von Schnitzel, commissario generale del Reich, e con gli industriali tessili dell'epoca furono decisive perché ricevesse l'incarico. Il progetto doveva recuperare il prestigio perso dalla Germania dopo la Prima Guerra Mondiale, e doveva servire da cornice alle attività diplomatiche ed ai contatti sociali propri di una fiera che promuoveva il commercio e le relazioni internazionali. Il padiglione fu eretto su un basamento rettangolare di 56,5 metri ed era delimitato da muri costituiti da un'armatura metallica con un rivestimento di marmo, slegati dal sistema strutturale dei pilastri, il che permise di ridurre la loro dimensione a 18 centimetri. La lastra del tetto appare molto leggera, visto che appoggia solo su otto pilastri cruciformi d'acciaio. Gli stagni poco profondi che occupavano parte della superficie, le chiusure in vetro e le pareti di marmo creavano una gran varietà di riflessi nell'edificio, che fu demolito poco dopo l'esposizione e fu ricostruito da Ignasi de Solà-Morales alla fine degli anni ottanta.

Tugendhat House

Cernopolní, 45
Brno, Czech Republic
1928–1930

The Greta Loew-Beer and Fritz Tugendhat matrimony owned a site in the Moravian town of Brno. The families of both marriage partners belonged to the textile bourgeoisie in the area. They exhibited culture and refinement and a certain tendency to want to modernize their surroundings, whether by means of their profession or through private friendships. The couple made contact with Mies thanks to the critic and collector of art Eduard Fuchs, who had already commissioned the architect to carry out an extension of the Perls house. The pronounced slope of the terrain made it possible to reduce the height of the building in relation to the street level by terracing the slope. On the access level, the children's rooms were installed, as well as those of the domestic service, the garage, and a large terrace with views of the city. Below this was the kitchen, the dining room (with a curved wooden wall), and the living room (divided in two by an onyx partition). The framing system uses cruciform columns of stainless steel inside, and galvanized columns outside. The relation with the surrounding natural environment is intensified by the transparency of the glass cladding and the reflections of the walls.

Le couple formé par Grete Loew-Beer et Fritz Tugendhat disposait d'un terrain dans la ville morave de Brno. Leurs familles respectives appartenaient à la bourgeoisie du textile de la région : cultivée, raffinée et affectant une certaine tendance à la modernisation de son environnement, au travers des relations professionnelles ou personnelles. Le couple entra en contact avec Mies grâce au critique et collectionneur d'œuvres d'art Eduard Fuchs, qui avait déjà commandé à l'architecte l'agrandissement de la maison Perls. La pente prononcée du terrain permit de réduire la hauteur de la construction, en regard du niveau de la rue, en recourant à des niveaux en terrasse. L'étage d'accès accueillit les chambres des enfants, les dépendances des domestiques, le garage et une grande terrasse dotée de vues sur la ville. Au niveau inférieur se situent la cuisine, la salle à manger délimitée par un mur en bois courbe et le salon divisé en deux par une partition en onyx. La structure est composée d'un système de piliers cruciformes, en acier inoxydable à l'intérieur et galvanisés à l'extérieur. La relation avec la nature environnante s'intensifie avec les transparences des vitres et les reflets des murs.

Das Ehepaar Grete Loew-Beer und Fritz Tugendhat besaß in dem mährischen Ort Brno ein Grundstück. Beide Familien gehörten zum gehobenen Mittelstand der Textilindustrie der Gegend: kultiviert, elegant, mit einer gewissen Tendenz zur Modernisierung ihrer Umwelt, sei es beruflich oder durch private Beziehungen. Das Paar nahm über den Kritiker und Kunstsammler Eduard Fuchs, der den Architekten bereits mit dem Umbau seines Hauses Perls beauftragt hatte, Kontakt auf. Durch die ausgeprägte Steigung des Grundstückes konnte die Bebauungshöhe bezüglich der Straßenlinie durch Terrassen auf den verschiedenen Ebenen reduziert werden. Im Eingangsgeschoss wurden Kinderzimmer, Räume für das Dienstpersonal, Garage und eine große Terrasse mit Blick auf die Stadt untergebracht. Auf der unteren Ebene lag die Küche, das Esszimmer – abgegrenzt durch eine gebogene Holzwand – und das Wohnzimmer – zweigeteilt durch eine Trennwand aus Onyx. Die Struktur besteht aus kreuzförmigen Pfeilern aus Edelstahl in den Innenräumen und galvanisiert in den Außenbereichen. Die Beziehung zur umgebenden Natur wird durch die Transparenz der Verglasungen und der Spiegelungen an den Wänden noch intensiviert.

I coniugi Grete Loew-Beer e Fritz Tugendhat possedevano un terreno nella località morava di Brno. Le famiglie di entrambi appartenevano alla borghesia tessile della zona: colta, raffinata e con una certa tendenza a voler modernizzare il proprio ambiente sia mediante la loro professione o attraverso le relazioni private. La coppia entrò in contatto con Mies grazie al critico e collezionista d'arte Eduard Fuchs, che aveva già incaricato l'architetto dell'ampliamento della casa Perls. L'accentuata pendenza del terreno permise di ridurre l'altezza della costruzione rispetto alla quota della strada, terrazzando i diversi livelli. Nel piano d'ingresso furono situate le camere dei bambini, le stanze di servizio, il garage ed una grande terrazza con vista alla città. Al piano inferiore si ubicò la cucina, il pranzo – delimitato da una parete curva di legno – ed il soggiorno, diviso in due da una separazione di onice. La struttura è formata da un sistema di pilastri cruciformi, di acciaio inossidabile all'interno e zincati all'esterno. La relazione con il paesaggio circostante è intensificata dalla trasparenza delle vetrate e dai riflessi delle pareti.

Farnsworth House

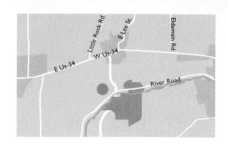

14520 River Road
Plano, Illinois, U.S.A.
1946–1951

Doctor Edith Farnsworth got in touch with Mies on the recommendation of the Museum of Modern Art (MOMA) of New York. She commissioned him with her project, a country house on a quiet rural site on the banks of the Fox River, some 80 kilometers from Chicago. Because the river overflows its banks frequently, flooding the site, a raised house was needed, and this was put on a platform atop eight steel columns painted white. The domestic spaces occupy a long bay with a rectangular base of 28 x 77 feet. The glass that comprises the only material in the façades reflects the surrounding area and also merges with the interior, making up an integral part of the activities in the house. It is a diaphanous interior space because the building was built as a perimeter structure only, with no other compartmentalization. The architectural language used in the pavilion in Barcelona pays off with maximum splendor in the Farnsworth House, generating a light, ethereal dwelling with a certain sense of the temporal. The differences that arose between client and architect regarding the budget and the way of working had to be resolved in court litigation and was finally decided in Mies' favor.

Die Ärztin Edith Farnsworth setzte sich dank der Empfehlung des Museums für Moderne Kunst in New York (MOMA) mit Mies in Verbindung und beauftragte ihn mit dem Bau eines Landhauses auf einem romantischen Grundstück am Ufer des Flusses Fox ungefähr achtzig Kilometer von Chicago entfernt. Da der Fluss das Grundstück häufig überschwemmte, musste ein hochgestelltes Gebäude geplant werden, das auf einer von acht weißgestrichenen Stahlpfeilern getragenen Plattform ruht. Die häuslichen Räume nehmen eine rechteckige Fläche von 8,5 x 23,5 Metern ein. Durch die vollkommen verglaste Fassade spiegelt sich die Umgebung in den Einfassungen wieder, fließt in den Innenraum hinein und wird zu einem Teil der Aktivitäten des Hauses. Der Innenbereich wirkt durchscheinend, da die Struktur an die Peripherie des Gebäudes verbannt wurde, ohne den Raum aufzuteilen. Die architektonische Sprache des Pavillons von Barcelona erfährt im Haus Farnsworth ihren größten Glanz in der Schaffung einer leichtwirkenden und ätherischen Wohnung mit einem gewissen Flair von Vergänglichkeit. Die Differenzen zwischen Kunde und Architekt anlässlich des Kostenvoranschlages und der Ausführung gelangten bis vor die Gerichte, die Mies schließlich freisprachen.

La docteur Edith Farnsworth contacta Mies sur recommandation du Musée d'art moderne de la ville de New York (MOMA) et lui confia le projet d'une maison de campagne sur un terrain bucolique, sur les rives de la rivière Fox, à quelques 80 kilomètres de Chicago. La rivière inondant fréquemment le terrain, il fut nécessaire de concevoir une demeure en hauteur, placée sur une plate-forme reposant sur huit piliers d'acier peints de blanc. Les espaces domestiques occupent un volume sur une base rectangulaire de 8,5 x 23,5 mètres. Le verre qui habille complètement les façades laisse l'environnement se refléter sur les ouvertures et, par surcroît, s'infiltrer à l'intérieur pour former partie intégrante des activités de la maison. Cet intérieur est diaphane, la structure ayant été reléguée sur le pourtour de la maison, offrant un espace sans compartiments. Le langage architectural, mûri avec le pavillon de Barcelone, acquiert toute sa splendeur avec la maison Farnsworth, engendrant une demeure légère et éthérée, avec une certaine touche de temporalité. Les différences ayant surgi entre le client et l'architecte, quant au budget et à l'exécution, menèrent les deux parties au tribunal qui rendit grâce à Mies.

La dottoressa Edith Farnsworth mise in contatto Mies su consiglio del Museo d'Arte Moderna di New York (MOMA), e gli incaricò il progetto di una casa di campagna in un bucolico terreno sulle rive del fiume Fox, a circa ottanta Km da Chicago. Poiché il fiume inondava frequentemente il terreno, si dovette progettare un alloggio soprelevato, posato su una piattaforma appoggiata su otto pilastri d'acciaio verniciati di bianco. Gli spazi domestici occupano un volume a base rettangolare di 8,5 x 23,5 metri. Il vetro che costituisce integralmente le facciate, permette che l'intorno si rifletta sulle chiusure e filtri anche all'interno, formando parte integrante delle attività della casa. L'interno è trasparente, visto che la struttura è relegata al perimetro della costruzione senza suddividere lo spazio. Il linguaggio architettonico sviluppato nel padiglione di Barcellona assume il suo massimo splendore nella casa Farns-worth, creando un alloggio leggero ed etereo, con un certo aspetto di temporalità. Le differenze che sorsero tra cliente ed architetto sul preventivo e sull'esecuzione giunsero in tribunale, che alla fine assolse Mies.

S.R. Crown Hall, IIT

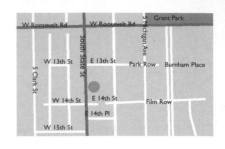

3300 South State Street
Chicago, Illinois, U.S.A.
1950–1956

Mies was the head of the architecture department at the Armour Institute when the organization merged with the Lewis Institute to create the Illinois Institute of Technology (IIT). The new group was a university that counted on a research center and that promoted above all the technological development of different disciplines. Mies was the architect of 22 of the institute's buildings, raised during the 1940s and 1950s, and among these is the outstanding chapel and the S.R. Crown Hall. This building houses the school of architecture and urbanism. The project is on a 120 x 221 foot plan and comprises two stories: a semi-subterranean section destined to the installations, and a large bay 18 feet high. The framework is made up of a large roof resting on steel columns that leave the ground floor free to distribute the interior spaces flexibly. This responds well to the changing needs of the university. The main entrance is by way of two flights of five steps joined by a granite podium. This is similar to the method used in the entrance to the Farnsworth house.

Mies war der Leiter der Abteilung für Architektur des Armour Institute, als dieses mit dem Lewis Institute fusionierte und das Illinois Institute of Technology (IIT) entstand, eine Universität mit einem eigenen Forschungszentrum, die in erster Linie die technologische Entwicklung verschiedener Disziplinen unterstützte. Mies war der Architekt von 22 der Gebäude, die das Institut während der vierziger und fünfziger Jahre baute; unter ihnen sind die Kapelle und die S.R. Crown Hall zu erwähnen, in denen die Architekten- und Städtebau-Schule untergebracht werden sollte. Das Projekt besteht aus einer Grundfläche von 36,5 x 67 Metern auf zwei Ebenen; einem Souterrain für die Anlagen und einem großen Raum mit 5,5 Metern Höhe. Die Struktur wird von einer großen, auf Edelstahlpfeilern abgestützten Decke gebildet, die den Raum für eine flexible Verteilung freigeben, so dass den wechselnden Anforderungen der Universität entsprochen werden kann. Den Haupteingang bilden zwei fünfstufige Freitreppen, die ähnlich der für den Eingang des Hauses Farnsworth verwendeten Lösung durch einen Granitsockel verbunden sind.

Mies était responsable du département d'architecture de l'Armour Institute lors de sa fusion avec le Lewis Institute pour créer l'Illinois Institute of Technology (IIT), une université comptant un centre de recherche et promouvant par-dessus tout le développement technologique de diverses disciplines. Mies fut l'architecte de 22 des œuvres que l'institution construisit au cours des année 40 et 50, parmi lesquelles l'on peut mettre en avant la chapelle et le S.R. Crown Hall, qui devait accueillir l'école d'architecture et d'urbanisme. Le projet consiste en un volume de 36,5 x 67 mètres de superficie et sur deux niveaux : un semi sous-sol destiné aux installations et un vaste espace de 5,5 mètres de haut. Le système structurel est formé par un grand toit reposant sur des piliers d'acier qui laissent l'étage libre afin que l'intérieur puisse être distribué de manière flexible, en répondant aux impératifs changeants de l'université. L'accès principal est fourni par deux escaliers de cinq marches unis par un podium de granite, de forme similaire à l'option retenue pour l'entrée de la maison Farnsworth.

Mies era il responsabile del dipartimento dell'Armour Institute quando questo si fuse col Lewis Institute per creare l'Illinois Institute of Technology (IIT), un'università che possedeva un centro ricerche incaricato di favorire primariamente lo sviluppo tecnologico di diverse discipline. Mies fu l'architetto delle 22 costruzioni che l'istituzione costruì durante gli anni quaranta e cinquanta, tra cui emergono la cappella e il S. R. Crown Hall, che doveva ospitare la scuola di architettura ed urbanistica. Il progetto si compone in un volume di 36,5 x 67 metri in pianta e di due piani: uno seminterrato destinato agli impianti ed un grande spazio di 5,5 metri di altezza. Il sistema strutturale è formato da una grande copertura appoggiata su pilastri d'acciaio che lasciano la pianta libera affinché l'interno possa essere distribuito in modo flessibile, rispondendo alle necessità mutevoli dell'università. L'entrata principale avviene attraverso due scalinate di cinque gradini unite da un basamento in granito, in modo simile alla soluzione utilizzata nell'ingresso della casa Farnsworth.

Promontory Apartments

Diversey & Sheridon Roads
Chicago, Illinois, U.S.A.
1946–1949

In 1946, Mies was working for the Illinois Institute of Technology (IIT) when he met the young promoter Herbert Greenwald. Greenwald had seen in Miesian structures the potential for the creation of economical dwellings. The project on Commonwealth Promenade was the first of six Greenwald commissioned Mies with between 1946 and 1949. The Wall Street crash of 1929 had strongly affected the construction sector, which did not recover until after the Second World War. The apartment tower the architect began to design in 1946 marked the first large-scale housing program carried out in Chicago and the first opportunity for Mies to develop a high-rise housing building. The shortage of steel panels caused by the war made it necessary to build in concrete. To save material and create a façade with a changing composite rhythm, the section was reduced to two columns every five floors, which produced a slight stepped effect. This strategy is emphasized by the exposed concrete frame. On the other hand, a marked difference was established between the simple, austere, lake façade and those looking onto the city with pronounced offsets.

En 1946, Mies travaillait pour l'Illinois Institute of Technology (IIT) lorsqu'il connut le jeune promoteur Herbert Greenwald, qui avait pris conscience des potentialités des structures de Mies pour la construction de logements économiques. Le projet de la Commonwealth Promenade fut le premier de six commandes que Greenwald allait confier à Mies entre 1946 et 1949. La crise de Wall Street de 1929 avait eu de graves répercussions sur le secteur de la construction, dont le rattrapage ne se produisit pas avant la fin de la Seconde guerre mondiale. La tour d'appartements que l'architecte commença à concevoir en 1946 constitua le premier programme résidentiel à grande échelle mené à bien à Chicago, comme la première opportunité de Mies pour développer les immeubles de logements en hauteur. Le manque de profils en acier, en raison de la guerre, obligea à construire en béton. Afin d'économiser les matériaux et de créer une façade dotée d'un rythme à la composition changeante, il fut nécessaire de réduire la section des piliers tous les cinq étages, produisant un léger effet d'échelonnement. Cette stratégie est encore en mise en valeur par la présence remarquée des poutres. D'un autre côté, fut instaurée une différenciation notable entre la façade donnant sur le lac, simple et austère, et celles s'insérant dans la ville, faites de retraits et de volumes.

1946 arbeitete Mies für das Illinois Institute of Technology (IIT), als er den jungen Bauherrn Herbert Greenwald kennenlernte, der die Möglichkeit bestätigte, die Strukturen von Mies für die Konstruktion von preiswerten Wohnungen zu verwenden. Das Projekt in der Commonwealth Promenade war das erste von sechs Aufträgen, die Greenwald zwischen 1946 und 1949 an Mies vergab. Die Krise an der Wall Street von 1929 wirkte sich durchgreifend auf den Bausektor aus, der sich erst nach dem 2. Weltkrieg erholte. Der Apartment-Turm, mit dessen Planung der Architekt 1946 begann, war das erste Wohnprogramm in großem Stil, das in Chicago ausgeführt wurde und bedeutete für Mies die erste Chance, ein Hochhaus für Wohnungen zu entwickeln. Der Mangel an Stahlprofilen infolge des Krieges zwang zu Betonkonstruktionen. Um Material einzusparen und eine Fassade mit wechselndem Aufbaurhythmus zu schaffen, wurde der Querschnitt der Pfeiler alle fünf Stockwerke verringert, wodurch der Eindruck einer leichten Abstufung erweckt wurde. Diese Strategie wurde durch das Hervorheben der Träger noch verstärkt. Andererseits wurde ein Unterschied zwischen der einfachen und strengen Fassade zum See hin und der stadtzugewandten Fassade mit Zurücksetzungen und Umfängen geschaffen.

Nel 1946 Mies stava lavorando per l'Illinois Institute of Technology (IIT) quando conobbe il giovane imprenditore Herbert Greenwald, che aveva intuito il potenziale delle strutture di Mies per la costruzione di alloggi economici. Il progetto nella Commonwealth Promenade fu il primo dei sei incarichi che Greenwald affiderà a Mies tra il 1946 e il 1949. La crisi di Wall Street del 1929 aveva avuto enormi ripercussioni sul settore delle costruzioni, che non si recuperò fin dopo la Seconda Guerra Mondiale. Il condominio che l'architetto cominciò a progettare nel 1946 era il primo programma residenziale su grande scala che si portava a termine a Chicago, e la prima opportunità per Mies di sviluppare un edificio per appartamenti in altezza. La scarsità di profilati d'acciaio dovuta alla guerra obbligò a costruire in cemento armato. Per risparmiare materiale e creare una facciata con un ritmo compositivo variabile, fu ridotta la sezione dei pilastri ogni cinque piani, il che produce un leggero effetto a scaloni. Questa strategia è enfatizzata dalla presenza in aggetto delle travi. D'altra parte, si creò una marcata differenza tra la facciata che dà al lago, semplice ed austera, e quelle che si addentrano nella città, con allineamenti e volumi.

Lakeshore Drive Apartments

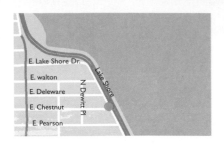

860-880 Lakeshore Drive
Chicago, Illinois, U.S.A.
1948–1951

After the Promontory Apartments, Herbert Greenwald and Mies again collaborated on a high-rise housing project that would prove to be a milestone of modern architecture. This was the first series of skyscrapers in the world made of glass and steel and thus initiating a new stage in the history of building. An advanced technology was used that did not add to the costs of the work because raising two towers was five percent less expensive than the average for this type in Chicago. The ingenuity of these projects is clear, from their siting on the trapezoidal terrain to the details of the cladding and the connection of the beams and columns in the skeleton. The whole is comprised of two towers that rise off two paved rectangles surrounded by vegetation. The particular location on the lakeshore provides the majority of the apartments with privileged views. Besides, the arrangement of the rooms inundates the spaces with natural light. The town ordinance in force in Chicago makes it necessary to fireproof the building. Thus, Mies created a system of rolled steel plates and other metal connectors as formwork for the concrete fireproofing.

Après les appartements de Promontory, Herbert Greenwald et Mies recommencèrent à coopérer avec un projet d'immeubles de logements en hauteur qui devraient marquer une tournant décisif dans l'architecture moderne : les premiers gratte-ciel du monde construits en acier et en verre, initiant une nouvelle étape de l'histoire de la construction. Le projet recourut à une technologie de pointe sans renchérir le coût de l'œuvre, le budget des deux tours demeurant 5 % sous la moyenne pour ce type de construction à Chicago. Le génie de ces projets est perceptible depuis la situation précise des édifices sur le terrain trapézoïdal jusqu'aux détails des fermetures et l'articulation de la structure. L'ensemble est formé par deux tours situées perpendiculairement sur deux surfaces rectangulaires pavées et entourées de végétation. L'emplacement particulier, sur les rives du lac, offre à la plupart des logements des points de vue privilégiés. Par surcroît, la disposition des pièces laisse la lumière naturelle inonder tous les espaces. Les normes municipales en vigueur à Chicago obligeaient à proposer certaines garanties de sécurité contre les incendies. Il fallut par conséquent concevoir un système de profils métalliques laminés servant de coffrage au béton de protection de la structure et sur lesquels vinrent se fixer les charpentes.

Nach den Promontory Apartments arbeiteten Herbert Greenwald und Mies erneut zusammen an einem Projekt für ein Hochhaus mit Wohnungen, das in der modernen Architektur einen Meilenstein setzte: die ersten Wolkenkratzer der Welt in Glas und Stahl, die eine neue Etappe in der Geschichte des Bauwesens einleiteten. Dazu wurde eine moderne Technologie eingesetzt, ohne dass dies eine Verteuerung bedeutete, wenn man bedenkt, dass die Kosten der beiden Türme 5% unter dem Durchschnittspreis für diese Art von Gebäuden in Chicago lag. Die Genialität dieser Projekte liegt in der Auswahl des richtigen Baugeländes auf einem unregelmäßig viereckigen Grundstück und geht bis hin zu den Details der Abschließungen und der Gestaltung der Struktur. Der Komplex besteht aus zwei vertikalen Türmen auf zwei rechteckigen, von Pflanzen umgebenen Flächen. Durch die bevorzugte Lage am Ufer eines Sees hat man von den meisten Wohnungen einen herrlichen Ausblick ins Weite. Die Räumlichkeiten sind so angeordnet, dass das Tageslicht alle Räume durchflutet. Da gemäss den in Chicago geltenden städtischen Bestimmungen Brandschutzgewährleistungen gefordert wurden, wurde ein System aus gewalzten Metallprofilen entwickelt, das zur Verschalung des Betons der Struktur diente und an dem die Elemente aus Holz befestigt wurden.

Dopo gli appartamenti Promontory, Herbert Greenwald e Mies tornarono a collaborare in un progetto per condomini in altezza che avrebbero segnato una pietra miliare nell'architettura moderna: furono i primi grattacieli del mondo costruiti in acciaio e vetro, iniziando così una nuova tappa nella storia delle costruzioni. Fu utilizzata una tecnologia avanzata che non fece rincarare l'opera, giacché il costo delle due torri si mantenne un 5% sotto la media di questa tipologia a Chicago. La genialità di questi progetti si percepisce sia dalla riuscita localizzazione delle costruzioni, che dai dettagli delle chiusure e dall'articolazione della struttura. L'insieme è formato da due torri collocate perpendicolarmente su due superfici rettangolari pavimentate e circondate di vegetazione. La particolare situazione sulle rive del lago permette che la maggior parte degli alloggi goda di una vista privilegiata. Inoltre, la disposizione delle stanze consente che l'illuminazione naturale inondi tutti gli spazi. La normativa vigente a Chicago obbligava a garantire la sicurezza contro gli incendi, così che si dovette studiare un sistema di profilati metallici laminati che servivano da cassaforma al cemento di protezione della struttura, ed al quale furono fissati i serramenti.

Seagram Building

Park Avenue & 53rd Street
New York, U.S.A.
1954–1958

At the age of 68, Mies accepted the commission to build the central headquarters of the company of Joseph E. Bronfman & Sons, a family business whose flagship business was Seagram's whiskey. Thanks to the recommendations of Phillip Johnson, who at that time was the director of the department of architecture of the MOMA, Samuel Bronfman trusted the project to Mies, who requested help from Johnson himself as supervisor of the work. The building was a 38-story skyscraper that would rise up as a unique element on Park Avenue. At the same time, the building would have to blend into the surrounding urban environment. A large granite dais was constructed to deal with the difference in grade between 52 Street and 53 Street, and the tower was set on the back of the site (in relation to Park Avenue). At the front of the terrain, two shallow ponds were placed symmetrically. The exterior was completed by the addition of garden areas around the glassed-in vestibule. The back part of the structure housed the Four Seasons Restaurant, designed by Phillip Johnson in 1957 and remodeled by Diller & Scofidio in 2000.

Mit 68 Jahren nahm Mies den Auftrag für den Bau der Zentrale der Gesellschaft Joseph E. Bronfman & Sons an, ein Familienunternehmen, dessen Geschäft die Herstellung des Whiskys Seagram war. Dank der Empfehlungen von Philip Johnson, der zu dieser Zeit der Leiter der Abteilung für Architektur des MOMA war, vertraute Samuel Bronfman Mies das Projekt an, der Johnson selbst darum bat, die Arbeiten zu überwachen. Es entstand ein 38stöckiger Wolkenkratzer mit Büros, der sich als einmaliges Element in der Park Avenue erhob und doch das umgebende Stadtbild respektierte. Um den Höhenunterschied zwischen den Straßen 52 und 53 auszugleichen, wurde ein großer Granitsockel gebaut und der Turm am Ende des Grundstücks errichtet, das im Vergleich zur Avenue zurückgesetzt lag. Im vorderen Teil der Parzelle wurden symmetrisch zwei flache Teiche angelegt. Außen wurde der Bereich um die verglaste Eingangshalle herum bepflanzt. Im hinteren Teil des Gebäudes befand sich das Restaurant Four Seasons nach einem Entwurf von Philip Johnson aus dem Jahr 1957, das im Jahr 2000 von Diller & Scofidio umgebaut wurde.

À 68 ans, Mies accepta une commande de construction du siège central de la société Joseph E. Bronfman & Sons, une entreprise familiale dont le fleuron était constitué par l'industrie du whisky Seagram. Grâce aux recommandations de Philip Johnson, alors directeur du département d'architecture du MOMA, Samuel Bronfman confia le projet à Mies, qui recherchа l'aide de Johnson pour la supervision des travaux. Un gratte-ciel de 38 étages de bureaux s'éleva comme un élément singulier sur Park Avenue tout en faisant montre de respect envers le tissu urbain environnant. Un vaste podium de granit fut disposé pour surmonter le dénivelé entre les 52ème et 53ème rues et la tour fut située à l'extrême du terrain, en retrait par rapport à l'avenue. Deux étangs peu profonds se disposèrent symétriquement sur la partie avant de la parcelle. Un parterre de végétation, tout autour de l'entrée vitrée, vint compléter l'extérieur. L'arrière de l'édifice accueillait le restaurant Four Seasons, projeté par Philip Johnson en 1957 et remanié par Diller & Scofidio en 2000.

A 68 anni Mies accettò l'incarico di costruire la sede centrale della compagnia Joseph E. Bronfman & Sons, un'azienda commerciale familiare il cui stendardo era l'industria dello whisky Seagram. Grazie alle raccomandazioni di Philip Johnson, che in quel momento era direttore dell'istituto di architettura del MOMA, Samuel Bronfman affidò il progetto a Mies, che chiese aiuto allo stesso Johnson perché soprintendesse i lavori. Fu eretto un grattacielo ad uffici di 38 piani che si innalzava come elemento singolare in Park Avenue, mentre si mostrava allo stesso tempo rispettoso del tessuto urbano circostante. Fu collocato un gran basamento in granito per superare il dislivello tra la 52ª e la 53ª strada, e si situò la torre nell'estremità del terreno arretrato rispetto al viale. Nella parte anteriore del lotto si disposero, in modo simmetrico, due stagni poco profondi. L'esterno fu completato con l'impianto di vegetazione attorno all'atrio vetrato. La parte posteriore della costruzione ospitava il ristorante Four Season, progettato da Philip Johnson nel 1957, che fu ristrutturato da Diller & Scofidio nel 2000.

Lafayette Park

1 Lafayette Plaisance
Detroit, Michigan, U.S.A.
1955–1963

Two and a half kilometers from the center of Detroit, Lafayette Park was the last project that Mies created for the promoter and builder Herbert Greenwald. The development was to regenerate a zone lacking in urban structures. Thus, the opportunity was there for putting into practice the idea of Ludwig Hilberseimer, a collaborator of Mies, of urbs in horto–arranging the dwellings in gardened space. Single-story houses with patio were mixed with two-story row houses and 21-story apartment buildings. In the center of the complex was a 20-acre green space, reached by pedestrian paths and catwalks that radiate from the buildings. The organization of the garden areas around the residences are reminiscent of the plan for the IIT campus. It was designed by Alfred Caldwell, one of Mies' fellow teachers at that institution. The parking areas were placed four feet below grade and traffic was limited to strict necessity. The quiet setting achieved allows users of the spaces a freedom from the hubbub usually found in large cities.

Zweieinhalb Kilometer vom Zentrum Detroits entfernt ist Lafayette Park das letzte Projekt, das Mies für den Bauherrn und Konstrukteur Herbert Greenwald durchführte. Ein Gelände ohne städtische Struktur sollte wiederhergestellt werden, und damit ergab sich die Möglichkeit, die Idee der "urbs in horto" des Freundes und Mitarbeiters von Mies, Ludwig Hilberseimer, in die Praxis umzusetzen; das hieß, Wohnungen in Gärten einzubetten. Vorhanden war ein Durcheinander von einstöckigen Häusern mit Hof, zweistöckigen Reihenhäusern und einundzwanzigstöckigen Apartmentblöcken. Im Zentrum des Komplexes wurde ein acht Hektar großer Garten angelegt, zu dem man von den Häusern aus über Wege und Fußgängerpfade gelangte. Die Gestaltung der Grünzonen, die die Wohnungen umgeben, erinnert an den Campus des IIT und wurde von Alfred Caldwell geplant, einem Kollegen von Mies an diesem Institut. Die Parkplätze wurden 1,2 Meter unter die Ebene der Gebäude verlegt und der Verkehr auf ein erforderliches Minimum beschränkt, so dass eine ruhige Atmosphäre ohne den Lärm der Großstädte geschaffen werden konnte.

Situé à deux kilomètres et demi du centre de Detroit, Lafayette Park fut l'ultime projet de Mies pour le promoteur et constructeur Herbert Greenwald. Le développement devait régénérer une zone dépourvue de structure urbaine, offrant l'opportunité de mettre en pratique l'idée Urbs in horto (la ville à la campagne), de Ludwig Hilberseimer, ami et collaborateur de Mies, consistant à disposer des logements dans un cadre paysager. Des maisons en patio et d'un seul niveau se mêlèrent à des résidences de deux étages en alignement et aux immeubles d'appartements de 21 étages. Au centre du complexe fut implanté un jardin de huit hectares, accessible par des chemins et des passerelles piétonniers sillonnant les édifices. L'organisation des espaces verts entourant les demeures n'est pas sans rappeler le plan du campus de l'IIT et fut projetée par Alfred Caldwell, compagnon d'enseignement de Mies dans cette institution. Les emplacements de stationnement furent abaissés 1,2 mètres sous le niveau des constructions, la circulation étant limitée au strict nécessaire. De là une atmosphère tranquille où les usagers se voient libérés du tohu-bohu propre des grandes villes.

Situato a due km. e mezzo dal centro di Detroit, Lafayette Park fu l'ultimo progetto che Mies realizzò per l'imprenditore e costruttore Herbert Greenwald. L'espansione doveva rigenerare una zona che era carente di struttura urbana, così che esisteva l'opportunità di mettere in pratica l'idea della urbs in horto, dell'amico e collaboratore di Mies Ludwig Hilberseimer, che consisteva nel disporre degli alloggi in un intorno trattato a giardino. Furono mischiate case ad un piano con giardino, alloggi a schiera di due piani ed edifici per appartamenti di ventuno piani. Al centro del complesso fu situato un giardino di otto ettari, al quale si accede attraverso sentieri e passerelle pedonali che aggirano le costruzioni. L'organizzazione degli spazi verdi che circondano gli alloggi ricorda il piano del campus dell'IIT e fu progettata da Alfred Caldwel, collega di docenza di Mies in questa istituzione. I parcheggi si interrarono 1,2 metri sotto il livello delle costruzioni e si limitò il traffico a quello strettamente necessario, il che riuscì a creare un ambiente tranquillo, dove gli utenti sono liberi dal frastuono proprio delle grandi città.

Neue National Galerie

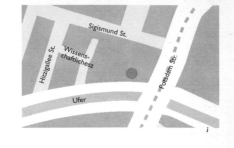

Postdamer Strasse, 50
Berlin, Germany
1962–1968

The only commission Mies received from the German government was to raise the Neue National Galerie. He employed the same type of pavilion as that used in projects such as the Barcelona one or the Farnsworth house. This structure was given a classical configuration with a modern order, a modern technology, and modern materials. The gallery had to include a large salon for temporary exhibits and small rooms for the museum's permanent collections. Moreover, it was necessary to add to this program offices, storerooms, workshops, and a garden to show sculptures. Making use of the site's slope, the auxiliary rooms and the garden were located at grade level, in fact a platform for the large exhibition space. A large metal roof on a column system covers a glassed bay interrupted only by the doors and the service apertures. The free, flexible plan is thus ideal for sharing the different functions for which the building was designed. The result is a building that slots into its environment in a special relationship and reflects the surrounding constructions, notable among which is the concert hall by Hans Scharoun.

La création de la Neue National Galerie fut l'unique commande reçue par Mies émanant du gouvernement allemand. Mies travailla sur la typologie du pavillon déjà utilisée pour des projets comme celui de Barcelone ou de la maison Farnsworth. Il la dota d'une composition classique avec un ordre, une technologie et des matériaux modernes. L'édifice devait abriter une grande salle d'expositions temporaires et de petites galeries pour les collections permanentes du musée. De plus, ce programme devait se voir ajoutés des bureaux, des entrepôts, des ateliers et un jardin d'exposition de sculptures. S'appuyant sur la pente du terrain, les dépendances et le jardin furent placés au niveau inférieur de la construction, servant de plate-forme pour les grands espaces d'exposition. Une vaste couverte structurelle métallique repose sur un système de piliers et recouvre un espace vitré dont les accès et les toilettes constituent les seuls volumes présentant une discontinuité sur un étage libre flexible : idéal à compartimenter de diverses manières selon les nécessités muséographiques. Il en résulte un édifice qui entretient une relation avec son environnement, reflétant les constructions avoisinantes, parmi lesquelles on relève la salle de concert de Hans Scharoun.

Der einzige Auftrag, den Mies von der deutschen Regierung erhielt, war der Bau der Neuen National Galerie. Mies arbeitete nach dem Vorbild des Pavillons wie schon bei den Projekten Barcelona und Haus Farnsworth, ein klassischer Aufbau mit moderner Technologie und modernen Materialien. Das Gebäude sollte einen großen Saal für wechselnde Ausstellungen und kleine Galerien für die ständigen Sammlungen des Museums enthalten. Abgesehen davon sollten zu diesem Raumprogramm Büros, Lager, Werkstätten und ein Garten für die Aufstellung von Skulpturen kommen. Die Steigung des Grundstückes wurde genützt und auf der unteren Ebene des Gebäudes die sekundären Räume und der Garten eingerichtet; diese Ebene dient gleichzeitig als Plattform für den weiten Raum, der den Ausstellungen vorbehalten ist. Eine große strukturelle Metalldecke stützt sich auf Pfeiler und überdeckt einen verglasten Bereich, in dem nur die Zugänge und Serviceeinrichtungen die freie und flexible Grundfläche unterbrechen, die jederzeit gemäß den ausstellerischen Bedürfnissen verschiedenartig aufgeteilt werden kann. Das Ergebnis ist ein Gebäude mit besonderer Beziehung zu seiner Umwelt, das die umgebenden Konstruktionen wiedergibt und dessen Konzertsaal von Hans Scharoun ganz besonders ins Auge fällt.

L'unico incarico che Mies ricevette dal Governo tedesco fu quello di costruire la Neue National Galerie. Mies lavorò con la tipologia del padiglione che aveva già utilizzato in progetti come quello di Barcellona o della casa Farnsworth, e la dotò di una composizione classica con un ordine, una tecnologia e dei materiali moderni. La costruzione doveva contenere una grande sala per mostre temporanee e piccole gallerie per le collezioni permanenti del museo. Inoltre, a questo programma si dovevano aggiungere uffici, magazzini, laboratori e un giardino per esporre delle sculture. Approfittando dell'inclinazione dell'area, si situarono le stanze di servizio ed il giardino al livello inferiore della costruzione, che agisce come piattaforma per il grande spazio espositivo. Una grande copertura in struttura metallica appoggia su un sistema di pilastri, e copre un perimetro vetrato nel quale gli accessi e i servizi sono gli unici volumi che interrompono una pianta libera e flessibile, ideale per essere suddivisa secondo le necessità espositive. Il risultato è un edificio che mantiene una speciale relazione col suo intorno, riflettendo le costruzioni circostanti, tra le quali risalta la sala per concerti di Hans Scharoun.

IBM Regional Headquarters

1 IBM Plaza
Chicago, Illinois, U.S.A.
1966–1969

The 58 stories of the office building for IBM's regional branch became the tallest of Mies' office buildings. The strict perpendicularity a work of these dimensions might take on was smoothed out through the use of various metallic bands at a point two-fifths of the total height and on the crown of the building. These courses cover the apartments and set the compositional pace for the façade. Like the major part of the skyscrapers Mies raised, this one is clad in glass and black-painted steel on a reinforced concrete frame. The light weight of the curtain wall contrasts with the vestibule walls, covered in large plates of travertine. Another Miesian touch is repeated on the ground floor: the stepped-back façade, which creates an overhang on the first floor and thus shades the access and traffic spaces. The project, one of the last effected by Mies, makes up part of the impressive architectural panorama on the shores of the Chicago River, in the center of the city.

Die höchste, von Mies durchgeführte Konstruktion ist das 58stöckige Bürogebäude für den Regionalsitz der Firma IBM. Die auffallende Vertikalität eines Gebäudes dieser Ausmaße milderte er durch Metallbänder, die in zwei Fünftel der Gesamthöhe und am oberen Abschluss (Krone) des Gebäudes verlaufen. Diese Streifen verdecken die Stockwerke für die Anlagen und bestimmen den strukturellen Rhythmus der Fassade. Wie die meisten der von Mies entworfenen Wolkenkratzer wurde auch dieser mit Glas und schwarzgestrichenem Metall als Verkleidung einer Struktur aus Stahl und Beton konzipiert. Die äußere Leichtigkeit steht im Gegensatz zu den mit Travertinplatten bedeckten Wänden der Eingangshalle. Im Erdgeschoss wiederholt sich ein weiteres typisches Detail von Mies: die Zurücksetzung der Fassade, wodurch das erste Stockwerk auskragt und Zugang und Verkehr beschattet. Dieses Projekt – eines der letzten von Mies entworfenen Gebäude – ist ein Teil des eindruckvollen architektonischen Panoramas am Ufer des Flusses Chicago im Zentrum der Stadt.

Les 58 étages de l'immeuble de bureaux destiné au siège social de la société IBM le convertissent en la construction la plus élevée réalisée par l'étude de Mies. La verticalité prononcée, par laquelle aurait pu pêcher une œuvre de ces dimensions, fut adoucie à l'aide de sentiers de bandes métalliques aux deux cinquièmes de la hauteur totale du bâtiment et en son sommet. Ces rubans couvrent les étages accueillant les installations et marquent le rythme de la composition de la façade. Comme la plupart des gratte-ciel projetés par Mies, celui-ci affiche des ouvertures vitrées et en métal peint de noir, qui recouvrent un système structurel en acier et en béton. La clarté de l'extérieur contraste avec les parois du hall d'entrée, habillées de grandes plaques de travertin. Une autre expression "miesienne" se répète au rez-de-chaussée : le retrait de la façade, le premier étage demeurant en projection et posant une ombre sur les espaces d'accès et de circulation. Le projet, un des derniers développés par Mies, s'inscrit dans un saisissant panorama architectural sur les rives de la rivière Chicago, au centre de la ville.

I 58 piani dell'edificio ad uffici per la sede regionale della compagnia IBM lo trasformano nella costruzione più alta di quelle realizzate dallo studio di Mies. L'accentuata verticalità che poteva raggiungere un'opera di queste dimensioni fu addolcita mediante strisce metalliche a due quinti dell'altezza totale e nel coronamento dell'edificio. Queste fasce coprono i piani degli impianti e marcano il ritmo compositivo della facciata. Come la maggior parte dei grattacieli progettati da Mies, anche questo ha una chiusura in vetro e metallo verniciato di nero che copre un sistema strutturale d'acciaio e cemento armato. La leggerezza dell'esterno contrasta con le pareti dell'atrio, che furono coperte da grandi lastre di travertino. Un altro aspetto tipico di Mies si ripete nel piano terra: l'arretramento della facciata, per cui il primo piano rimane in aggetto e fa ombra agli spazi di accesso e circolazione. Il progetto, uno degli ultimi che sviluppò Mies, forma parte del magnifico panorama architettonico sulle rive del fiume Chicago, nel centro della città.

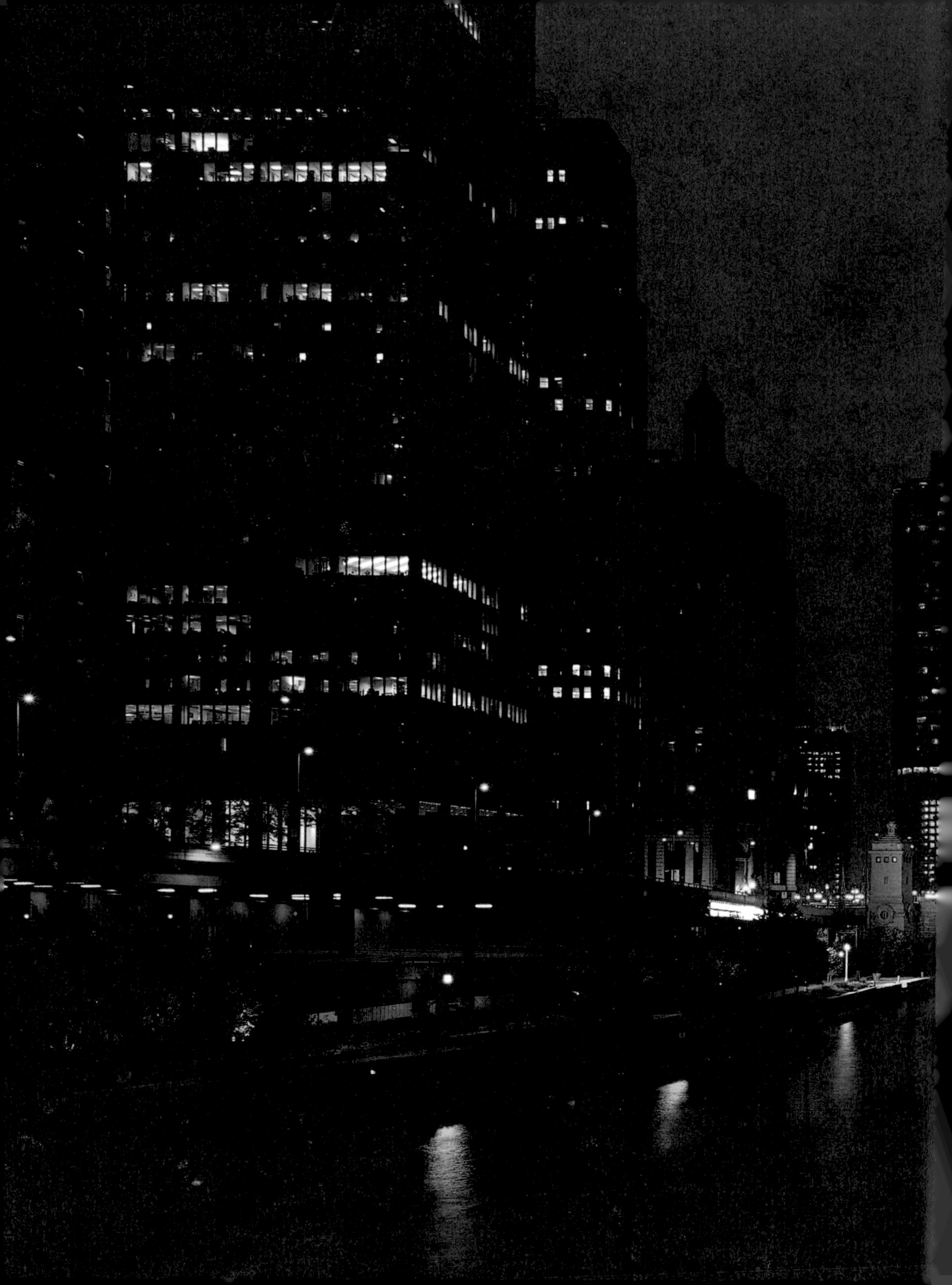

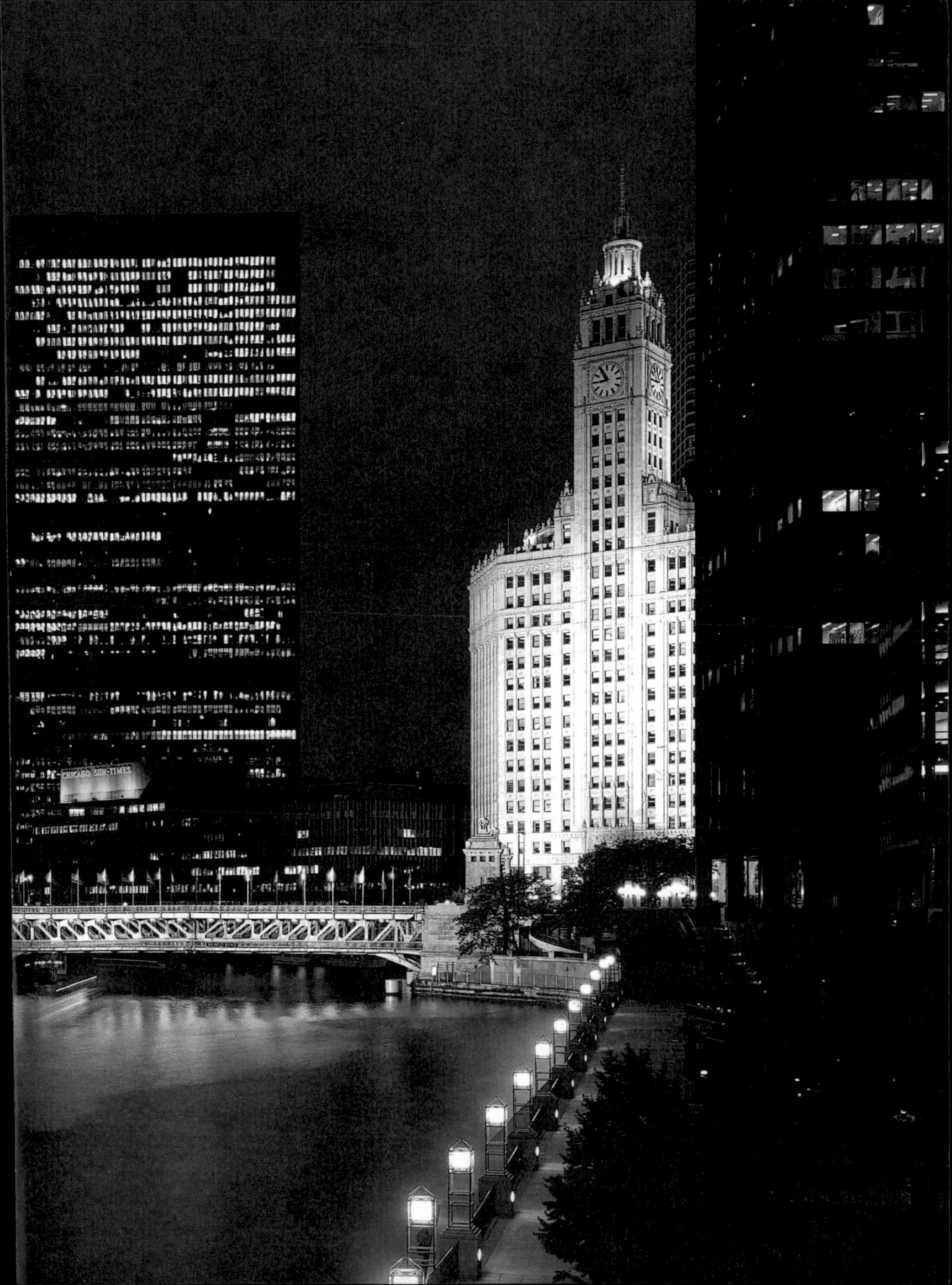
CHICAGO SUN-TIMES

Chronology of Mies van der Rohe works

1907	Riehl House, Potsdam-Babelsberg, Germany
1910	Project: Bismarck Monument, Bingerbrück-Bingen, Germany
1910–1911	Perls House (later Fuchs House), Berlin-Zehlendorf, Germany
1912	Project: Kröller-Müller House, Wassenaar, The Netherlands
1912–1913	Werner House, Berlin-Zehlendorf, Germany
1914	Project: House for the Architect, Berlin-Werder, Germany
1914–1915	Urbig House, Berlin-Neubabelsberg, Germany
1919	Monument for Laura Perls, Berlin, Germany
1921	Project: Friedrichstrasse Office Building 1, Berlin, Germany
	Project: Petermann House, Berlin-Wilemsdorf, Germany
1921–1922	Feldmann House (demolished), Berlin-Grunewald, Germany
1922	Kempner House (demolished), Berlin-Charlottenburg, Germany
	Project: Glass Skyscraper
	Eichstaedt House, Berlin-Wannsee, Germany
1922–1923	Project: Concrete Office Building
1923	Project: Concrete Country House
	Project: Lessing House, Berlin-Neubabelsberg, Germany
	Project: Ryder House, Wiesbaden, Germany
1923–1924	Project: Brick Country House
1924–1926	Project: Mosler House, Berlin-Neubabelsberg, Germany
1925	Project: Dexel House, Jena, Germany
	Monument for Alois Riehl, cemetery in Neubabelsberg, Berlin, Germany
1925–1927	Wolf House (destroyed), Guben, Poland
	Weissenhof Housing Colony and Exhibition, Stuttgart, Germany
1926	Monument to the November Revolution (Karl Liebknecht-Rosa Luxemburg Monument), (destroyed), cemetery, Berlin-Friedrichsfelde, Germany
1926–1927	Municipal Housing Development on the Afrikanische Strasse, Berlin
1927	Apartment Building, Weissenhof Housing Colony, Stuttgart, Germany
	Glass Room, Exhibition at the Gewerbehallenplatz, Stuttgart, Germany
	Silk Exhibit (Exposition de la Mode), Berlin, Germany
1927–1930	Esters House, Krefeld, Germany
	Lange House, Krefeld, Germany

1928	Project: Adam Department Store, Berlin, Germany
	Project: Bank Building, Stuttgart, Germany
	Project: Remodeling of Alexanderplatz, Berlin, Germany
1928	Fuchs House (formerly Perls House), Berlin-Zehlendorf, Germany
1928–1929	Project: Friedrichstrasse Office Building 2, Berlin, Germany
	German Pavilion, German Industrial Exhibits and German Electricity Pavilion (demolished in 1930 and rebuilt in 1986, under the supervision of Ignasi de Solà-Morales), Barcelona Exposition, Spain
1928–1930	Tugendhat House, Brno, Czech Republic
1929	Project: Nolde House, Berlin-Zehlendorf, Germany
	Kiosc for the German Linoleum Works, Building Fair, Leipzig, Germany
1930	Project: Golf Club, Krefeld, Germany
	Project: War Memorial, Remodeling of Interior of K.F. Schinkel's Royal Guardhouse, Berlin, Germany
	Addition to Henke House, Essen, Germany
	Crous Apartment, Berlin, Germany
	Ruhtenberg Apartment, Berlin, Germany
	Hess Apartment, Berlin, Germany
1930–1935	Johnson Apartment, New York, USA
	Factory Buildings for the Vereinigte Seidenwebereien AG (Verseidag), Krefeld, Germany
	Project: Court Houses
1932	Project: Gericke House, Berlin-Wannsee, Germany
	Remodeling of Bauhaus, Berlin-Steglitz, Germany
1932–1933	Lemke House, Berlin-Hohenschönhausen, Germany
1933	Decoration of Bauhaus for Carnival Ball, Berlin-Steglitz, Germany
	Project: Reichsbank, Berlin, Germany
1934	Project: Service Station on the highway, Germany
	Glass and Mining Exhibits, Deutsches Volk / Deutsche Arbeit Exposition, Berlin, Germany
	Project: Mountain House for the Architect
1935	Project: Hubbe House, Magdeburg, Germany
	Project: Ulrich Lange House, Krefeld, Germany
1937	Lohan Apartment, Rathenow, Germany
	Project: Verseidag Administration Building, Krefeld, Germany

1939	Preliminary Campus Plan, Armour Institute of Technology, Chicago, USA
1940–1941	Master Plan, Illinois Institute of Technology (IIT), Chicago, USA
	Kaufmann Department Store Displays, Pittsburg, USA
1942	Project: Museum for a Small City
1942	Project: Concert Hall
1942–1943	Metals Research Building for Armour Research Foundation, IIT Research Institute, Chicago, USA
1944	Project: Library and Administration Building, IIT, Chicago, USA
1944–1952	Engineering Research Building for Armour Research Foundation, IIT Research Institute, Chicago, USA
1945	Studies: Classroom Buildings, IIT: Metallurgy, Physics and Electrical Engineering, Chemical and Civil Engineering, Architecture, Humanities, Gymnasium and Swimming Pool, Chicago, Illinois, USA
1945–1946	Alumni Memorial Hall, IIT, Chicago, USA
	Metallurgial and Chemical Engineering Building (Perlstein Hall), IIT, Chicago, USA
	Chemistry Building (Wishnick Hall), IIT, Chicago, USA
	Project: Cantor Drive-in Restaurant, Indianapolis, USA
1945–1950	Boiler Plant, IIT, Chicago, USA
1946	Exhibition of José Guadalupe Posada, The Art Institute of Chicago, Chicago, USA
	Promontory Apartments, Plano, Illinois, USA
1946–1947	Project: Cantor House, Indianapolis, USA
	Central Vault, IIT, Chicago, USA
1946–1951	Farnsworth House, Plano, Illinois, USA
1947	Exhibition of Mies van der Rohe, Museum of Modern Art, New York, USA
	Exhibition of Theo van Doesburg, Renaissance Society, University of Chicago, Chicago, USA
1948–1950	Association of American Railroads Administration Building, IIT, Chicago, USA
1948–1951	860-880 Lake Shore Drive Apartments, Chicago, USA
	Interior, The Arts Club of Chicago, Chicago, USA
1948–1953	Mechanical Engineering Building for the Association of American Railroads, IIT, Chicago, USA
1949–1952	Chapel, IIT, Chicago, USA
	Bard College Dormitories, Annandale-On-Hudson, New York, USA
1950	Project: Caine House, Winnetka, Illinois, USA
	Project: Chicago Beach Apartments, Chicago, USA
	Revision in Stainless Steel of Barcelona Exposition Furniture and Tugendhat Chair

1950–1956	S. R. Crown Hall, IIT, Chicago, USA
1954–1958	Seagram Building, New York, USA
1955–1963	Lafayette Park, Detroit, USA
1959–1963	Home Federal Saving and Loan Association of Des Moines, Des Moines, Iowa, USA
1959–1964	Federal Center, Chicago, USA
1960–1961	Project: Schäfer Museum, Schweinfurt, Germany
1960–1963	Project: Friedrich Krupp Administration Building, Essen, Germany
	One Charles Center, Baltimore, USA
	2400 Lakeview Apartments, Chicago, USA
	Lafayette Towers Apartment Building, Detroit, USA
	Project: Milbrook Commercial Center, Newark, USA
1961	Project: Mountain Place, Montreal, Canada
1962	Project: Pavilion Recreation Area, Detroit, USA
1962–1965	Meredith Memorial Hall, Drake University, Des Moines, USA
	Science Center, Duquesne University, Pittsburgh, USA
	Social Service Administration Building, University of Chicago, Chicago, Illinois, USA
1962–1965	Highfield House Apartment Building, Baltimore, USA
1962–1968	Neue National Galerie, Berlin, Germany
1963	Lafayette Towers, Lafayette Park, Detroit, USA
1963–1969	Dominion Center, Toronto, Canada
1964–1966	Project: Foster City Apartment Development, San Mateo, California, USA
1964–1968	Westmount Square, Montreal, Canada
1965–1968	Martin Luther King Memorial Library, Washington D.C., USA
1966	Master Plan, Church Street South, New Haven, Connecticut, USA
	Project: K-4 School, New Haven, USA
1966–1969	Brown Wing, Museum of Fine Arts, Houston, USA
	IBM Regional Headquarters, Chicago, USA
1967	Project: Mansion House Square and Office Tower, London, England
1967–1968	ESSO Service Station, Nun's Island, Montreal, Canada
1967–1969	Highrise Apartment Building No. 1, Nun's Island, Montreal, Canada
	Project: King Broadcasting Studios, Seattle, USA
1967–1970	111 East Wacker Drive, Illinois Central Air Rights Development, Chicago, USA